I0441528

MY STRUGGLE

MY STRUGGLE

DAVID HULT

Copyright © 2016 by David Hult.

ISBN: Softcover 978-1-5144-3812-1
eBook 978-1-5144-3811-4

All rights reserved. No part of this book may be reproduced or transmitted in any form or by any means, electronic or mechanical, including photocopying, recording, or by any information storage and retrieval system, without permission in writing from the copyright owner.

Any people depicted in stock imagery provided by Thinkstock are models, and such images are being used for illustrative purposes only.
Certain stock imagery © Thinkstock.

Print information available on the last page.

Rev. date: 01/13/2016

To order additional copies of this book, contact:
Xlibris
1-888-795-4274
www.Xlibris.com
Orders@Xlibris.com
732377

CONTENTS

Part one: The president will issue an executive order, to hold elections in the new year:

Have a referendum election, with both, a proposed change to a new constitution, a new Congress, new vice president, and a new president.

To create a New National License Bureau (NLB). The NLB will register, everyone to vote and issue a national identification card. This card will be used to vote, get a job, and all transactions, etc.

To create an expanded CBO. The CBO will be the gatekeeper's, for providing, a balanced budget, and paying down the debt, 2% annually.

Part Two: Balance the budget and pay down the debt.

Part Three: A world-class K-12 school system, and college with free tuition. Pay off all student loans and end the loan program.

Part Four: A Supreme Court, that makes it a priority to protect America's constitutional rights. Their action should be proactive, not sit back and wait for constitutional issues to come to them, but rather, the court finds problems and corrections.

Part Five: Bring back the draft.

Part Six: A listing, of additional items, that we should be doing.

Part Seven: Create a public works program, for relocating, retraining, educating, and the certifying level of work skills and then arrange to hire in the public sector. A program to Replace, our existing unemployment program.

Part Eight: We should change the American flag, to a single large bold, white star, on a solid light blue background, indicating our national unity as a country and as a people. Change the national anthem to God bless America so people can sing the national anthem.

Part one

THE PRESIDENT SHOULD ISSUE AN EXECUTIVE ORDER, FOR A REFERENDUM ELECTION, IN THE NEW YEAR

We will expand the duties of the newly created National License Bureau. The NLB will handle our national elections, our national opinion polls, and our national referendums.

The NLB will also issue a national identification card for every voter, and all voters must register to vote or face a fine. The NID will be used on many occasions: voting, getting a job, and all financial transactions, etc.

We will expand the duties of the newly created CBO. The CBO will be our gatekeeper, for regulating the nation's revenue and ensuring not only a balanced budget but that we reduce the national debt as well.

The national referendum. Will, provide the voters a chance to create laws. If the voters have a 51% approval, on one of the NLB's many opinion polls, then it will become law. That 51% is 51% of the total voters from the last election. Pure democracy in action.

Every quarter, all voters, will upgrade their individual information at the NLB: voting preference, polling preference, and national referendum preference. Failure to do so will result in a fine.

Anyone is receiving political donations, asking for, or giving donations, is subject to a felony conviction. Ending political donations will smash the glass ceiling between Congress and the American people.

The CBO will finance our elections, and no longer the billionaires and corporations, with their political donation bribes.

Each senator will represent, 1% of the population and have the dual title of Senator and Governor.

Each senatorial district will have four congressional districts, of equal population. The representative, in each of the four districts, will have the dual title, of representative and Mayor.

All members of Congress, live in their home districts, 80% of the time or more. This country will have a total of 100 governors and 400 mayors.

We are eliminating our worthless Congress, Senate, and State Governments. We will no longer be representing and supporting the billionaires and corporations. The government will be supporting the nation and the majority of people. We will have a representative form of government.

We will have a national referendum where people can vote and create laws.

We are eliminating, politically, state governments and the two-party system. Neither of these two entities has served the interest of the majority of Americans.

All voters, at or over, the age of 18, can run for any office, and stay in office, as long as they have a 51% approval rating or better per the NLB. The voters will include, legalized citizens, naturalized citizens, and citizens in prison.

Anyone that is actively trying to deny people the right to vote will be subject to a treason conviction.

Our Founding Fathers flirted with making owning property, a requirement for voting, but threw it out, because they decided, voting was a standalone right, and should not have any pre-requisitions.

Republicans, are trying to convince us, that voting is a privilege, rather than a right. Republicans, use this line, to justify voter suppression, which should be an act of treason.

The Senate will deal with national and international issues, as, it is a collection of governors. The House will deal with internal issues, city issues, as it is a collection of mayors.

Most bills will go through either, the House or the Senate. On an exception basis, a bill can go through both houses, if requested.

When the Senate passes a bill, it needs only the president's signature to become law. When the house passes a bill, it requires both the vice president and the president's signature to become law.

The president can fill all his national appointments and then the Senate can review his choices, by approving or disapproving, with a 51% vote. An effort to reduce all the games played in Congress rather than helping the country and the majority of people in the country. A game that serves no purpose.

If a person, wants their name on the ballot, they must apply to the NLB and have an approval rating of 5%, or more, per the NLB. All politicians must apply to the NLB if they want to run for office.

Multiple names will appear, for the same position on the ballot. The same name can be on both the president and vice president's ballot. The person wins both, and then it is their choice, as to which one to take.

At the top of the list, is the person with the highest percentage approval rating, and then, down to the lowest rate no party affiliation, will appear on the ballot. Neither, will the two-party system be on the ballot.

The CBO will come up with options, balancing the budget, paying down the debt and present these options to the president for his approval and then to the Senate for review.

A 1-year green card, which allows a person to have a driver's license, pay taxes, and have no arrest record, and be in the process, of learning English. Failure to comply will result in deportation.

A 5-year green card, as all the rights of a one-year, and also, as thank you very much a path to citizenship. Also, they must demonstrate a working knowledge of English. A series of test, both oral and written examinations, developed and used. Failure to comply will result in a review by the NLB and even deportation.

All green card carriers must report to the NLB, on a quarterly basis.

The national government will assign, a series of agents, to deal personally with all green card carriers. If an officer, finds fault, then they will submit their complaint to the NLB, for review and possible action.

All green card carriers will also have a national identity nation card, from the NLB.

Green card carriers can vote on national referendums, and opinion polls, but, not for people running, for political office.

Obama care should be replaced, with a single-payer Medicare program. The insurance companies, with Obama care, take one dollar [out of every five (20%) for themselves. The VA hospitals have an overhead percentage that is between 3% to 5%.

Healthcare should be a right, along with voting, and neither do have a profit margin attached to them to exploit people.

The reduced cost is because, they are government run. The country should make an effort, to eliminate all medical insurance programs, because it's an unnecessary cost to the voters. Half the country lives in poverty and 30% weave in and out of poverty over the lifetime. 80% of the population will benefit, from a single-payer system.

We should expand the VA. Have the CBO, finance and run, a program for expanding VA type hospitals. Hospitals, with their lower overhead cost, will also provide lower-cost for the public. This will be a big help for 80% of the population, who needs help.

Veterans should be an issue a national medical card, for obtaining health care, drugs and care at other facilities.

The CBO will pay the cost of the cards. The CBO will also pay the cost of building and buying hospitals as needed.

Have the CBO use tax dollars to set up the government-funded single-payer system and cover the cost of stabilizing and getting it going. Then, make the single-payer fund self-sustaining without tax dollars.

The fund should be open, to all ages.

The standard Medicare program will remain intact, for all those 70 years of age or more.

We need a national website; that displays the voting record and actions, of all people holding public office. The website will also define their political stripes.

When Republicans, win national elections, the rich get richer by paying little or no taxes, Corporation pay no taxes and get subsidies and a reduction in regulations. Reduce regulations mean dirtier air, dirtier water, and dirtier soil.

With Republicans, there is no hope they will balance the budget because they believe in the deficit. Use the deficit as both an excuse and a means to eliminate social benefits for many needy Americans.

The looting of the country will get worse, 50% are now in poverty, and that will increase, 30% weave in and out a poverty over the lifetime and that number will increase.

The Republicans are trying to turn this country and to Central American Banana Republic. Where a handful of people are multibillionaire's and the rest run around barefooted.

When the Democrats, gain power, the past feel-good legislation without adequate funding. Like affirmative action. Like the mainstream education act that was supposed to be hundred percent funded.

The maximum funding on any given year is about 30%. They are also good about passing fragmentation legislation. They have no overall plan to make this country a better place to live in.

The reason I wrote this book is because middle America does not have a political party that represents them and we have a broken political system, that neither party wants to fix.

Part Two

Balance the Budget and Pay Down the Debt

Eliminate the business tax. Eliminate all tax deductions. Redo all subsidies. The new subsidies will focus on the national needs, for helping the maximum number of people. Stop taxing American's and American companies overseas.

No longer, will the government provide subsidies and special tax cuts for billionaires and corporations. The government will redirect these kinds of efforts, to make this a stronger nation, for the majority of Americans.

Reinstate the progressive income tax, from 2% to 30%. A progressive consumption tax from 2% to 10%. Remove the glass ceiling, from Social Security tax. Have a progressive Social Security tax from 2% to 10%.

Raise the age for Social Security and Medicare to 70 years of age. At 70, you get 30% of the benefits both Social Security and Medicare. Every year after, you get a 10% increase, and it's 77 you get hundred percent and Medicare.

Initially, there will be a 30% increase Social Security benefits.

Bring back the inheritance tax. Those receiving, the inheritance will be subject to both the progressive income tax and the progressive consumption tax with no deductions.

At the time of a person's death, all assets will be frozen. Including insurance policies. Then, releasing the death certificate will be done by the IRS. A person from the IRS will sign off on the death certificate. Everything will be in included in his financial evaluation: insurance policies, records for paying taxes on the homes and cars, etc.

The IRS will use, for their evaluation, the value of the home for the tax bills.

The interior of the house will be estimated at half the value of the home. The recipients, if they object, for any reason, then all assets will be sold.

The bill of sale will be taxed at the progressive income tax of 2% to 30%. The CBO will advise on the various levels of tax. No lawyers will be involved.

If those who received the funds have any complaint, they should contact the NLB and state their grievance. If they have a valid grievance, the NLB will send the grievance to a judge.

This program is a benevolent redistribution of wealth. Everyone should give back a portion of what the country has given to them. So we can build a first-class nation: livable minimum wage, free tuition and land grant type colleges and universities, the best K-12 school system in the world, national healthcare, national mental health care, energy independence, address climate control, etc.

If you earn money, then you pay taxes to Social Security. Social Security tax will fund all social programs. If necessary, it will also add funds to the single-payer Medicare system as a temporary, or permanent backup plan.

Expand the duties of the CBO, as they will be the gatekeeper for plans to raise 102% of the revenue for the budget. Every quarter we pay the national debt by 1/2 of 1%, or 2% a year.

The federal government will provide the funding for all governors and mayoral districts in the country. The governors and mayors will submit a budget to the CBO, for cost evaluation and setting standards. This proposal goes to the president for his approval and then to the Senate for review. Now we have a solid unanswered base for this country. We can start doing things for this country and the majority that people, rather than subsidizing the billionaires and large corporations.

The CBO should install natural gas pumps, all along the interstates and in the 30 largest cities. The CBO to build a single smart power grid and replace the three obsolete power grids that we have. All non-nuclear power plants will run on natural gas. Lower electrical cost and cleaner air.

Today a single nuclear power plant runs twice a day at peak efficiency 3 to 6 hours and producing the maximum power plants produce the lowest-cost electricity during the peak running time. Today these plants produce 24% of our total electricity.

Spain built a huge power for wind and solar, that produces enough energy for 90 homes. We should build at least 15 of these in the Southwest.

We have a crash program, to find a process, making coal and acceptable fuel source. We close, all underground coal mines and enter the coal miners into our two-year relocation retraining, re-education and jobs in the public sector.

The smart power grid, will run these nuclear plants at peak efficiency and produce 48% of our electricity. Lower cost electricity and cleaner air. We eliminate, all coal burning facilities. All these items will give a boost, to our emerging natural gas industry.

We need a single-payer system for Social Security.

At the age of 70, Social Security and Medicare will get 30% of the benefits, 71 40%, etc. when the new system, goes into effect, a 30% increase across the board for Social Security will happen.

All those over 77 will not pay and get hundred percent reimbursement for Medicare. Under 70, the CBO will set up and run the single-payer system. After the system is set up and running the people paying into the system will be the ones paying for it. If we choose, the CBO could pay some percentage to the system to reduce the cost to the consumer. The percentage could go from 0% to 100%.

Part Three

A WORLD-CLASS K-12 SCHOOL SYSTEM. NATIONALIZE LAND GRANT TYPE COLLEGES AND UNIVERSITIES

K-12 and colleges will have free tuition. The expensive tuition college and universities will not be included in this program. Any expensive program that is reduced and matches the land grant then will be included.

School-wide individual competition. Eliminate team sports. Individual competitions, will include swimming, diving, track and field, golf, handball, luminosity, Microsoft solitary collection etc.

Pay off all student loans and end the loan program.

The parents and students will pay half the cost of the teachers' pay in our world-class school system.

Parents and students will hire, fire, and negotiate salaries for teachers, eliminate team sports and have a school wide individual competition with a variety of subjects, including academics Competition.

All scores posted. At each level, there will be three levels of skill. Also, there will be a male division and a female division.

School starts at 9 AM and ends at 8 PM. Teachers will work either "A" shift or "B" shift. Overtime pay as needed.

Preschool and kindergarten will be set up along the lines of homeschooling. A teacher's aide will have 2to 4 students, and a teacher will have as many teacher's aides as are required.

After the students have had, keyboarding, then, they will start being assigned workstations (computers). These workstations will be used to receive a national broadcasting of all required subjects.

Workstations will provide a series of interacting programs, testing, grading and recording the grades. The computer will then forward the grades to the front office or mainframe.

Students will swipe their national student identification card at the keyboards, as part of the login process. All students will register at the NLB.

The national public school system will broadcast three academic levels, for required subjects, every school day.

Pay off all student loans. End the student loan program.

Schools will be laid out as a University with a single principle.

Schools will be year-round. Nine weeks in school and three weeks off. The school will close for maintenance for weeks a year. Or, two weeks every six months.

During the first hour of school is meet, greet and have breakfast. Homeroom, for 20 minutes in the first hour. Students can come earlier. Mirrors are arranged, all along the halls and cafeteria.

The second and third hour is for competition in sports activity and academic competition and the last two hours will be the same.

Required subjects will use the computers. Computers timeslots will be 4-5 hours as needed.

Electives will attend stadium style seating classrooms, and all subjects will be in a time slot of 1 to 3 hours or more as needed.

Parents and students can pick their electives the class-size. And, if they want an all sexes class, or one's sex class can have it, a religious teacher can teach a religious class with opening and closing for all. The only requirement is that all students in the classroom, have the same religion.

In the event, that the parent's criteria will add a financial impact, then the parents will pay the difference in cost. We want the electives to be all-inclusive and open to whatever the parents want.

One of the electives will be ROTC. Anyone who completes the ROTC course will enter the service with a three level pay grade. They will also be eligible for office or school. The three level pay grade starts at the end of three months of basic training.

My English speaking son and his wife used this system on our two grandchildren. It took 200 hours to teach basic reading and writing and 400 hours of basic math mice son spoke only Spanish to them until they started first grade. It took two hours to teach them basic speaking and reading Spanish. I believe, speaking a foreign language that you are teaching, is important and effective

My two grandchildren had a significant advantage over other students all through K-12. All students should have this benefit.

My granddaughter at a full ride at Truman state. Also, $4,000., For travel allowance in Europe in the summertime. My grandson is a junior in high school, he does well in school but comes in second to his sister.

The criteria for passing the first grade has already been discussed. Any foreign language will work. No social promotion.

Today, for every 15 students entering kindergarten, ten will graduate from high school. Three of the students qualify for college, and one will graduate. A disgrace to this country. We can and should do better.

We have at least three different groups of students attending K-12: college-bound students, not college bound students but work at grade level, and students who cannot work at grade level.

During, preschool, and kindergarten, though students who cannot pass will be put in the group that cannot work at grade level. On an annual basis, students in this group will be reviewed to confirm their assigned level. Parents who are unhappy with this assignment can ask for reevaluation at any time. It is possible that a student in this category can work at grade level in some subjects are assigned there. That is part of the evaluation on an annual basis.

The school system should and well, meet the needs of all three levels using customizing class scheduling.

We also need two parallel paths, for college-bound students. One route is math and science, and English is with technical writing and minimum of humanities: sociology, psychology, philosophy, etc. Many shop courses. This group will have a concentration on math and science. Some in this group will go for a BS degree at a college or university.

And those are not working at grade level. Both groups should qualify for an entry-level job, upon graduation from high school. The school's should seek employer's input, on the kinds of teaching and what level to ensure their properly trained before graduating in school.

The third group is a path for a BS degree and will be heavy into humanities and liberal arts.

The schools will provide swimming pools, tennis courts, chess rooms, reading rooms, band rooms, handball rooms and outdoor 3

Wall Courts, a track. And, all students will learn and participate in all the sports.

Team sports is an elective and competition between the teams will compete on Saturday. The appropriate coaching will be used.

Students will wear icons on their clothing, indicating their competitive levels of achievement. Dress code strictly enforced. Same dress code for all students.

Schools will provide three meals and snacks.

The parents will pay transportation to school and home. Dress code clothing provided by the CBO.

Saturday's could be used for testing and competition as required. Students and parents will pay half the cost of teacher's pay. They will also hire and fire and agree on an annual salary for all the staff including the principal. The CBO will pay the cost of brick-and-mortar, utilities, food, land, repair cost, etc.

A national broadcasting system will dispense the facts. The broadcast will go directly to individual workstations.

Each student will have a customized workload according to their ability. They may be in one grade level for English and a different grade level for math. A series of workstations assigned to teacher's aides. A group of computers assigned to a teacher's aide will be for two as a pod. Several pods. Will be assigned to a single teacher.

The broadcast, on the same subject, will have three levels, to address the three level of students. The programs will be set up for interactive study and grading. The workstation will record the grade's; the student must get a perfect grade. Or, the student will have to retake the same test to achieved a perfect grade. Failure to do so will result in a review of the student status.

The computer will also assign homework. Homework completed in school. Teacher's aides will assist homework assignments as needed. A specific time for all students will be for doing their homework.

Parents are in charge of the demographics of the classroom and decide the number of students a teacher has. All students will wear a national identification cards around their neck at all times uniforms paid for by the federal government.

All complexes will have the correct number of police officers, nurses, computer technicians, building maintenance, etc. the police will monitor the halls and incoming and outgoing of the complex.

Any student may request to be removed from the family and live on the school campus the system should be designed to improve the students living conditions for all students in an effort should be made to encourage students from slum areas to live on campus. Students will be pulled, to make sure the home environment is up to standards. When they find a problem situation, they will encourage the students to leave home and stay in the complex.

I think this is the most important thing we can do for the country is getting our children on the correct, safe, tranquil path for a better life and education too many children today live in homes and locations that prevent them from having a secure future, and I believe this will correct that.

Parents may also request that a student lives in the housing includes problem children.

Students living on campus will have a per diem for clothing and other expenses we should break the bonds of students living in slums or from troubled homes and treat them to a secure and safe environment.

If a young girl becomes pregnant, then she will remain in school and live in the housing unit if she so chooses. If a young man has acted inappropriately, he will be sent to the VMI program. If he still misbehaver's, then he will be sent to juvenile detention.

Housing will be provided for both students and educators to eliminate the need for busing.

Encourage parents, teachers and teachers' aides to be paid counselors in these housing units.

We also will have a VMI (Virginia Military Institute) type compounds and schooling for students with disciplinary problems and students who cannot work at grade level. The system will have a high degree of discipline and respect for teachers and teachers' aides. The teachers will have the authority to remove the students from the classroom and even from the school system if necessary. They can also recommend changing her status. Any parent accosts a teacher in an angry, or inappropriate way will result in the student being removed from the school system. Principles have no contact with teachers; their job is to run the school and pay the bills. The teachers are in charge.

There will be a teacher's review board manned by teachers and headed by the principal. Parents can go and address their concerns to this group. The principal will have the final word.

Any student in this category who refuses to live full-time on campus and engage in this program will be dismissed from the school system and barred from returning for at least one year. At that time, a reevaluation will be done.

One of the activities of the VMI group will be competitive marching in groups. These groups will also engage in Indian walking: the last person in line runs to the front of a line and when they arrive the front battalion goes to the next runner.

Each group's time posted on boards.

Students teachers and teachers' aides are free to move to new locations and transportation will be provided.

The principles pay may not exceed hundred and 50% of the highest teacher's pay.

The principle must maintain a 51% approval rating of the teachers or lose their job. Teachers maintain a 51% approval rating of the parents and students or lose their job.

Anyone who is working in this country that has people working for them, must maintain a 51% approval rating for two-quarters or lose their job the 51 approval rating applies to all leadership positions, and the military included.

All students will be screened and tested for mental health problems. And, if necessary, spend some time in a mental health facility to determine what treatment is necessary. Part of the treatment will be mandatory testing to ensure that the patient is taking the drugs at all times. Failure to do this will result in further confinement. The screening testing confinement and mandatory testing to ensure a person is taking the drugs will be our national mental health program for the whole population the CBO will run and fund the program.

Affirmative loaners program. These young males who commit these mass shootings have several things in common. Never dated a girl. Never kissed a girl and were virgins. It appears to me that a social paranoia against everyone develops with these people. And, anger and frustration, follow.

I think schools, should screen these kids, to find a group of ALP'. When this group is identified, arrange for an in-school dance, involving just them and find other activities that this group can do. Put on plays, eat together in the cafeteria and always arrange boy, girl, boy, etc. in the seating.

Their homework: they have to learn the names of everyone in the group and be tested on that. They have to be given three names of both sexes with their phone numbers, and they have to call these people and talk to them for no less than two minutes. And keep rotating names. Then write an essay of what they found out about these people. I think this group needs structure in dealing with people of the opposite sex.

Another homework assignment: Sadie Hawkins Friday night dating. A girl must ask a boy of her choosing out, and he must accept. The following Friday, the boy, must ask a girl of his choosing out on Friday night, and she must accept her head at me. The following Friday, Sadie Hawkins double dating. The next Friday it will be the guys for double dating.

Maybe form a bowling league. The schools could have bowling lanes. All teams must be half girls and boys. If possible, arrange pods with only ALP's and classrooms.

The ALP's are the prime target of school bullies. This group should constantly be screened and obtain the names of the bullies. There should be some form of school discipline for boys like VMI program.

Part Four

A Supreme Court will make it a priority to protect America's constitutional rights

Their action should be proactive, not sit back and wait for constitutional issues to come to them, but rather the court should find problems and solutions.

The Supreme Court will serve at the pleasure of the president. The president may add or subtract judges at will.

When the Supreme Court makes a ruling, then this decision will go to the CBO for cost evaluation. And then, to the Pres. for approval and then, to the Senate for review with a 51% approval/disapproval.

Part Five

Bring back the draft

All males on their 18th birthday should report to the draft board for six months of Marine style basic training.

For the first three months, all Marine style basic training all day.

And the second three months will be divided between half-day Marine training and the afternoon will have academic studies.

At the end of six months, the recruits will be assigned a branch of military service they can leave active duty after six months serve for additional two years in the reserves or National Guard.

They can finish high school in the military for one year at a school has an ROTC program. After completing the six months course and the schooling, they will have a pay grade of level III.

They can stay in the service and graduate college and come out a Second Lieutenant and serve an additional four years.

Other options are possible.

During the six months, two hours each day must be devoted to competition in both physical and academic endeavors. Three levels of competition. Everyone's name will be on the charts with their results:

They will engage in competitive swimming, diving and swimming, tennis, volleyball, field and track, marching competition, martial arts, running, Lumosity, Microsoft Solitaire collections, Chess and team sports of all kinds, etc.

An effort will be made to ensure that all trainees can compete in each of these areas for at least one time, after that, they can settle in for three or four activities of their choosing.

Part Six

THE FOLLOWING IS A LIST OF THINGS WE SHOULD DO.

We will replace our unemployment system with a public works program: PWP, the unemployed will go through a two-year program that includes education, retraining and relocation to find jobs. During that time, they will also be members of the PWP.

We should empower the nurses. When I was at the VA and requested a heart doctor, I was met with a nurse. The nurse acted as a screener and made sure I needed to see the doctor. The public sector should adopt this policy for all doctors and pay the nurses that are acting as screeners 75% of the doctor's pay.

Academic courses should be set up for a senior nurse position, to act like a doctor's aide. There are many routine things that the doctor does, but a trained nurse could do, and should do.

We should empower the pharmacies. In England, pharmacies can do refills without calling a doctor. The doctor prescribes the medication and the amount of medication and after that, the pharmacies take over.

We should empower the post office to become financially and independent of financial aid. We all pay the same postage, when it comes to service, we subsidize the wealthy and business for deliveries. That should change.

The only free mail service should be those that have a string of mailboxes altogether. After that, the cost of delivery should be prorated depending on the service and charged with a monthly fee.

All project listed below and above will also use PWP workers as needed.

As a country, we should look for ways to become more inclusive, more supportive, and more empowering for the voters. Compare that to what the state governments is doing to us now.

Public corporation's members may not serve on the Board of Directors. The Board of Directors needs a maintain a 51% approval rating from the shareholders and members of the Corporation. All president and vice president positions must maintain a 51% approval rating from both the Board of Directors Shareholders and members of the Corporation.

Public corporations seal salary may not exceed 100 times the salary of the lowest paid employee. If a company, has a manufacturing site overseas, the lowest paid employee will be the base for the CEOs salary.

Any bonus programs will include for all employees. Any profit-sharing programs will include for all employees. Middle managers are subject to a 51% approval rating by the group they are managing. Failure to do this will cause them to get fired. Middle managers should have at least 30 employees working for them.

Anyone in this country, who has authority over other people, must maintain a 51% approval rating. If they go for two-quarters, consecutive quarters, and fall below the 51% approval rating, then they should be removed from office. No exception! Let's get rid of bad bosses.

The police force should have a 51% approval rating from the community that they serve. If not, the voters can fire the police department. Or, selectively replace some individuals. All police departments should have the same demographics as the community they are serving. Any community has a right to decide its criteria for hiring police officers. Even if it means hiring convicted felons. We should eliminate trial by jury's because our racial and religious bias keeps us from doing a good job. We should get rid of all prosecuting attorneys because their vested interest in never prosecuting a bad cop prevents them from doing a good job. And replace both with three judges.

Judges should offer compensation to the victims. We should introduce justice into our justice system. The courts can seize the material and wealth and selling it and give the proceedings to the victims.

These judges will go through a training course based on their community's needs. The judges must also maintain a 51% rating with the communities they serve in.

When a trial starts, one judge will act as prosecuting attorney, and the judge will act as a defense attorney. The third judge will decide the case independent of the two other judges. The three judges will decide among themselves, how to handle future cases.

We should have more paying jobs, more jobs, in prison half the money they earn goes to the victims. In the case of guilty murderer's, the judge can pick how much compensation and sell the convicts wealth and pay it to the victims.

The federal government will make sure that our regulatory and inspection agencies are fully funded. We should have the correct amount of individuals needed to keep this country's air, water, food, and banks in top-notch shape this job will be the shared responsibility between the CBO, the president of the United States, and the Senate.

Break up the big banks and make them each four regional banks and have them independent of each other and improve our rules for regulation. Make sure no financial institution can buy and sell stocks. Only loans.

Simplify and reduce our spy agencies, and agencies personnel, and put them under a single leader. Reduce the number computer jockeys and increase the number of field agents.

In the war on drugs and legalize drugs. Allow, the growing distribution, and selling of drugs in this country. The federal government Will regulate the growing, selling and distribution program. Federal permits are required at each step in the process. The permits will be issued and purchased in each death by the CBO. All funds will go to the federal government.

Free-trade has been great for the billionaires and corporations and a disaster for the working class.

Mexico has fewer jobs at lower wages because of free-trade. Most countries involved have the same results. We should end blanket free trade agreements and go to fair trade as needed. China, should not be a free-trade country and must be on the fair trade deal each country will be judged on its merit, the criteria will be equal trade dollars per population.

Japan. Who has one-third our population? Therefore, each dollar trade Japan buys from us, we, in turn, will buy three trade dollars with Japan, etc. we will have free trade with Japan under those circumstances and any other country.

Part of Seven: create a public works program for relocating retraining, certifying and locating jobs in the public sector for these people.

Workers will enroll in the PWP at a pay rate of $15 an hour. The CBO will send out a contract, like a military contract, to cover the cost.

Let's say the contract is for cutting down trees. So the contract is sent to several businesses that cut down trees for this project. They will hire unemployed workers, veterans, underground coal miners, parolees, and make sure they become proficient in all phases of the work. We should close all underground coal mines and have a crash program to create a process that will make coal a desirable fuel source.

One of the conditions of the PWP is that the person who takes the contract must hire at least one of the workers for a year.

Another contract might be to assist farmer. All along the interstates, we have land between the two lanes. The government will sell farmers a lease describing one of these plots of land. The land outside of the two lanes and on the side.

The farmer has the option of being the first bidder. If he accepts what the government is asking, then the land will be leased to him. If the farmer turns down this offer or does nothing for six months, then this plot will be open for bids.

The government can dictate which crops to grow in the highways grass lanes.

The program eliminates the mowing cost of grass along the interstate highways and provides more farm land for the farmer.

The PWP will assist the farmer with cutting down of trees, removing fences and making the land a more desirable place to plant crops and thereby increase the acreage for farming. The government will pay the PW workers, and it will not cost the farmer anything.

If the farmer has other tree lines on his property and wants to tear them down so we can plan additional crops, the PWP will do this also. All workers must be trained in every facet of this project and certified that they are proficient. A grade will be given to the PWP workers, and that grade will appear on the certificate at the office of PWP. The workers fired; they cannot join PWP for one year. PWP will also have an appeals court.

PWP employers may dictate the grade level they wish to hire.

If the farmer wants a barn built, the PWP will do that. Add a fence, or repair a fence, but they must hire at least one worker for a year.

Pay of C grade is $14 an hour, B grade is $15 an hour and for and a grade it is $16 an hour. A running tally will be done by the PWP to figure grade average. Anything less than a C, then the person is dropped from the program for one year.

Home builders, plumbers, or electricians, also use this service on the condition that they certify and hire at least one worker for one year.

The fast food industry can also hire PWP's.

If a manufacturer once to expand their labor force, then the PWP will fill the bill, on the condition, that the manufacturer will hire one or more of the workers, when they are proficient, certified and accepted.

If a state is having a natural disaster, say a forest fire, they can call for PW P workers. And, again, the workers must be proficient at every job that is involved to be certified.

The forest service may wish to create a healthy forest from the overcrowded forest. They must hire at least one or more workers who obtain the certification.

A state or city may ask for trash pickup along the interstates. In the program today, principles volunteer their teachers to do it for nothing. Again, certification will be done, and the states must provide a job. The government will cover the relocation cost of the employees, and the new employer must hire those workers at $15 an hour.

The unemployed, veterans, underground coal miners will be the first shot at these jobs. Jobs not filled will be filled with open enrollment.

We will end all outsourcing of jobs out of the country. Instead, a company may propose a project to the government. In that proposal, the employer will estimate how many workers are needed. The PWP workers will be used at no cost to the employer until the plant is up and running for one year. The CBO will pay the cost of the land and supply the PWP workers to construct the plant at no cost to the employer. The CBO will offer a low-interest loan for equipment, etc.

The employer, can interview the PWP workers and pick those he wishes to hire. The employer must fill his staff with PWP workers. The employer can insist on all grade "A" workers at every level. If none is found, then open enrollment.

The president should issue an executive order, for anyone in prison who has not committed a violent crime, cannot serve more than six months. No one in prison can serve more than ten years. All prisoners and parolees will be subject to the national mental illness program with its condition that if you fail to take the drugs that are automatic confinement.

We should abolish capital punishment. A felony conviction will not bar people from running for office or any other job, but they must inform their new employer of their conditions and details of their conviction. We cannot have prison reform and rehabilitation as long as we have these absolutes.

We should nationalize the military industrial complex and make all members a special branch of the National Guard.

That way we can reduce the 50 billion we spend on weapons the military does not use or want. The special guard can lay off workers, who will enroll in the National Guard and receive two weeks a year training in the military complex.

Make an effort to close, somewhere around 100 overseas bases that can best be described as World War II type bases.

If we want to have a base in another country, then they need to have a base in our country. End the occupation mentality. We should invite Russia and China to participate in this program.

We should invite several foreign countries, to participate in our hundred zones political system: Canada, Ireland, England, Australia, New Zealand, Poland, all EU countries, and Japan.

We should end all military aid to other countries.

We should stop all aid of any kind to Israel because we are their friends, and they are not our friends. When it comes to Arabs in their country and the and the treatment of these Arabs is very close to how the Nazi Germany treated the Jews.

That said we should offer all Jews and Arabs in Israel dual citizenship. Also, offer free transportation to this country, if they do not feel safe in the Jewish state. I think that Netanyahu is a thug and should go back to selling used cars.

We prize Jewish Americans for outstanding academic and business achievements. My quarrel is with the state of Israel: because they have not offered a comprehensive peace proposal to the Arabs and the surrounding states. Also, there treatment of Arabs within

Israel as second-class citizens. Israel should become the EU of Arab states and provide equal status for Arabs.

We should empower whistleblowers. If a whistleblower, loses their job over reporting a malfeasance, and the report proves reliable, then the whistleblower should receive all back pay to that date. Also, the whistleblower will receive an additional ten years pay.

If a person is found guilty of a malfeasance, then all property associated with that individual will be seized and sold for compensation to the victim.

If there is a victim, the judge will reward the victim with the proceeds. If no victim is involved, then the proceeds will pay towards their incarceration.

Anyone in charge of a group is legally responsible for what malfeasance their activities during working hours. If one of his subordinates, commits a malfeasance, then the superior has two choices: testify against their subordinate or expect the same punishment as the subordinates get, in that case, the business will be sold to pay for the incarceration.

The president should issue an executive order: any church that preaches politics from the pulpit will lose its tax-free exemption. The Constitution spells out the separation of church and state and we should enforce it.

Any politician who advocates religious items or policies should be called before a judge and fined. The individual should be fined $10,000 and not paid from campaign funds. The political party that the fined person represents will pay a fine of $1 million. And again, no campaign money should be used. The receipts were given to the judge.

We should bring back sedition laws. Anyone who earns a living trying to divide the country, or run the government, is guilty of treason. They should be placed in front of the judge and fined $10,000 or more. The fine doubles for a repeat offender. If they represent an organization, then the organization will be fined $1 million. This kind of message poisons the political process, and it is time this incident.

People can criticize the government, but they cannot earn money doing it.

The NLB, and have some phone banks dedicated to calls from college and university girls who have been raped. They will provide their name (it will never be used in the public) and the name of the person or persons who did the raping, school, date of the rape and time of day. If they know the name of the department associated with the rapist, include that. The Rape victim should include the story of how the school treated her, and that will be included in the listing of schools.

Any girl raped in this country will be included in this program. Provide your name, give as many details about the accused rapist as possible, when, where, is he married and who, what does he work, what time a day. Tell us in detail, what the police told you and what they did or didn't do. The NLB will provide a list for non-college girls along with all the details of the alleged victims.

The NLB will calculate, Rapes per capita for each school and post this listing the school and the names of the accused rapist.

The NLB will also serve as an appeals court for an alleged rapist. They will turn over this evidence to a judge forwarding.

All marriages and all couples who want to live together must register at the NLB. When a couple divorces, that divorce must be registered at the NLB. If the man should move, change jobs, etc., he must inform the NLB of changes.

If a wife, informs the NLB that she is not getting the financial support from her ex-husband, then the NLB will take the appropriate action.

We should extend the Mississippi River an additional 40 to 60 miles along the coast of Mississippi and Alabama. The Mississippi will do a 90° bend and enter a channel 40 to 60 miles going east. At the start of the channel, with will be equal to the width of the Mississippi at that point. At the end of the channel, the width will be Twice the width of the Mississippi.

Channel locks will be built alongside the Mississippi near the entrance of the channel, so ships can enter and exit the Mississippi River.

We should build, a rock and concrete wall along the shores of Louisiana, to stop the land erosion. The PWP will direct and build a series of fish farms and rice farms in both Louisiana and Mississippi. They will populate these fish farms with members of the PWP.

We should cover, all interstates, with a layer of asphalt to reduce both noise and increase miles per gallon.

The president should issue an executive request for churches," I believe in mass prayer. Sometimes, during the service have the audience pray in unison for the president to give the president the wisdom and the courage to do what is best for the country and pray for peace.

Our pipelines are exploding. I believe they are Van de Graaff generators producing large static charges and that causes the explosion. The pipes are new and clean they are grounded. As they become corroded they lose this ground connection. We need to insert a self-cleaning copper rod into the oil stream.

In the Great Lakes and oceanfront's, we should build an arch of large wind tunnels equally spaced. The inside of the arch faces the shoreline. We should connect the base of the wind tunnels to each other and the shore for support.

We should build a man-made coral reef made of polypropylene and weight with rocks. The bottom layer should have small holes. The second layer should have slightly larger holes etc. in cross-section, it will look like a pyramid. A wire will run through each box and connect to the base of the wind turbine at each end.

This will also be a fish sanctuary.

We should have a department of Internet security. Both the defensive and offense of plans and preparations. We should actively engage shutting down countries that attack us.

Part of Eight

WE SHOULD CHANGE THE AMERICAN FLAG, TO A SINGLE BOLD WHITE STAR ON A SOLID LIGHT BLUE BACKGROUND INDICATING OUR UNITY

www.ingramcontent.com/pod-product-compliance
Lightning Source LLC
Chambersburg PA
CBHW030546290526
45786CB00004B/1881
* 9 7 8 1 5 1 4 4 3 8 1 2 1 *